Dragons

Dragons

Fearsome Monsters from Myth and Fiction

GENERAL EDITOR:

GERRIE McCALL

an imprint of
SCHOLASTIC
www.scholastic.com

Published by Tangerine Press, an imprint of Scholastic Inc.,
557 Broadway; New York, NY 10012

Scholastic Canada
Markham, Ontario

Scholastic Australia Pty. Ltd
Gosford, NSW

Scholastic New Zealand
Greenmount, Auckland

Scholastic UK
Coventry, Warwickshire

10 9 8 7 6 5 4 3 2

ISBN-13: 978-0-545-01319-2
ISBN-10: 0-545-01319-4

Editorial and design by
Amber Books Ltd
Bradley's Close
74-77 White Lion Street
London N1 9PF
United Kingdom
www.amberbooks.co.uk

Project Editor: Sarah Uttridge
Design: Talking Design
Illustrations: Myke Taylor/The Art Agency

Printed in Singapore

Picture credits: All © Amber Books Ltd.
Jacket, front: Beowulf's dragon
Jacket, back: Futs-Lung

Contents

Introduction

Dragon encounters have been reported throughout the world. Many experts dismiss dragons as entirely mythical, explaining them away with claims that belief in dragons is a case of mistaken identity. These experts theorize that the discovery of dinosaur fossils led to the invention of the dragon. People gazing upon dinosaur bones for the first time must have imagined an animal fabulous enough to deserve such bones and came up with the dragon. However, many credible eyewitnesses describe contact with dragons. Marco Polo encountered them during his travels and Leonardo da Vinci drew pictures of them. Legend says that Alexander the Great was the son of a dragon. Even Chinese and Japanese emperors of the past believed they were descendants of dragons.

Dragons of the world are as varied as the cultures to which they belong. Dragons are awesome creatures with or without wings. Depending on their country of origin, a dragon can play the role of guardian, nuisance, creator, or destroyer. There are the benevolent dragons of Asia who demand respect and offerings, as well as the deadly fire-breathers of Europe who demand human sacrifices. Generally, dragons are revered in the East and feared in the West.

One reason why dragons hold the imagination is because so many of them breathe fire. In fact, they are the only creature with the ability to shoot flames. This is just one of the dragon's fascinating traits that allow it to live on in legend across the globe. In a world where it seems everything has been researched and cataloged thoroughly, the dragon remains refreshingly elusive. Lack of scholarship in this area leaves the field of dragon study wide open for new discoveries, whether they be in ancient accounts or in face-to-face meetings with the wondrous beasts.

Beowulf's Dragon

WINGS
Batlike wings attached to the torso by robust muscles lift the dragon in flight. The bones within the wing structure are hollow to reduce their weight.

TAIL
The barbed tail shaped like an arrowhead can be used as a weapon in battle. In flight, the tail operates like a rudder, balancing the dragon and allowing it to execute skillful aerial maneuvers.

EYES
Adapted to see in the dim light of caves, the dragon's eyes are well suited for watching over its hoard of plundered treasure.

JAWS
Its fiery breath lights the skies. Chain mail provides no defense against its crushing jaws and poisonous fangs. A reservoir of venom is located in the upper jaw.

BODY
The dragon's enormous body is blackened by the soot of its own flames. Its blue-green scales glow with inner fire.

Coiled in a cavern beneath a gray rock there is a terrifying dragon—a fire drake measuring 50 feet (15 m) long. The dragon guards a lair filled with piles of priceless treasure. Its heavy body blocks daylight from reaching the armor, goblets, jewels, coins, and golden swords it hoards deep in the cave. When a thief steals a golden cup from its lair, the dragon rampages through the countryside, burning everything it sees. The fire drake breathes flames that light up the sky, terrifying villagers and burning every home in Geatland. Beowulf, King of the Geats, armed with a magic sword, leads an army into battle to face the dragon.

ACTUAL SIZE

▶ BEOWULF STRIKES THE DRAGON WITH HIS SWORD, but the blow glances off the beast's terrible hide. Beowulf is engulfed in dragon flames, a sight so terrifying that his army flees. Only the faithful Wiglaf remains to help. Beowulf breaks off the blade of his magic sword in the dragon's head. Bitten on the neck by the dragon, Beowulf is soaked in his own blood but continues fighting. Wiglaf stabs the dragon in a vulnerable place and Beowulf slashes it through the middle, cutting the monster in two and ending its life.

Where in the world?

Geatland, a region in the south of Sweden, is where Beowulf met the mighty dragon in battle. Geatland's deep forests provided the ideal habitat for a fire drake.

Did you know?

- Beowulf dies from his battle wounds. The dragon's treasure is removed from the cave and buried with Beowulf. All the pieces of the dragon's corpse are thrown into the sea.
- The dragon's flames are so intense that they burn Wiglaf's shield down to its handle. Wooden shields, such as the one Wiglaf used, are a poor choice when doing battle with a fire drake.
- Beowulf carries an iron shield bearing the image of a dragon.
- A dragon's lightweight bones are tougher than reinforced concrete.
- Smoke rising from the mouth of a cave is usually a tell-tale sign that a dragon resides within.
- The dragon is the largest-known flying creature.

Gorynych

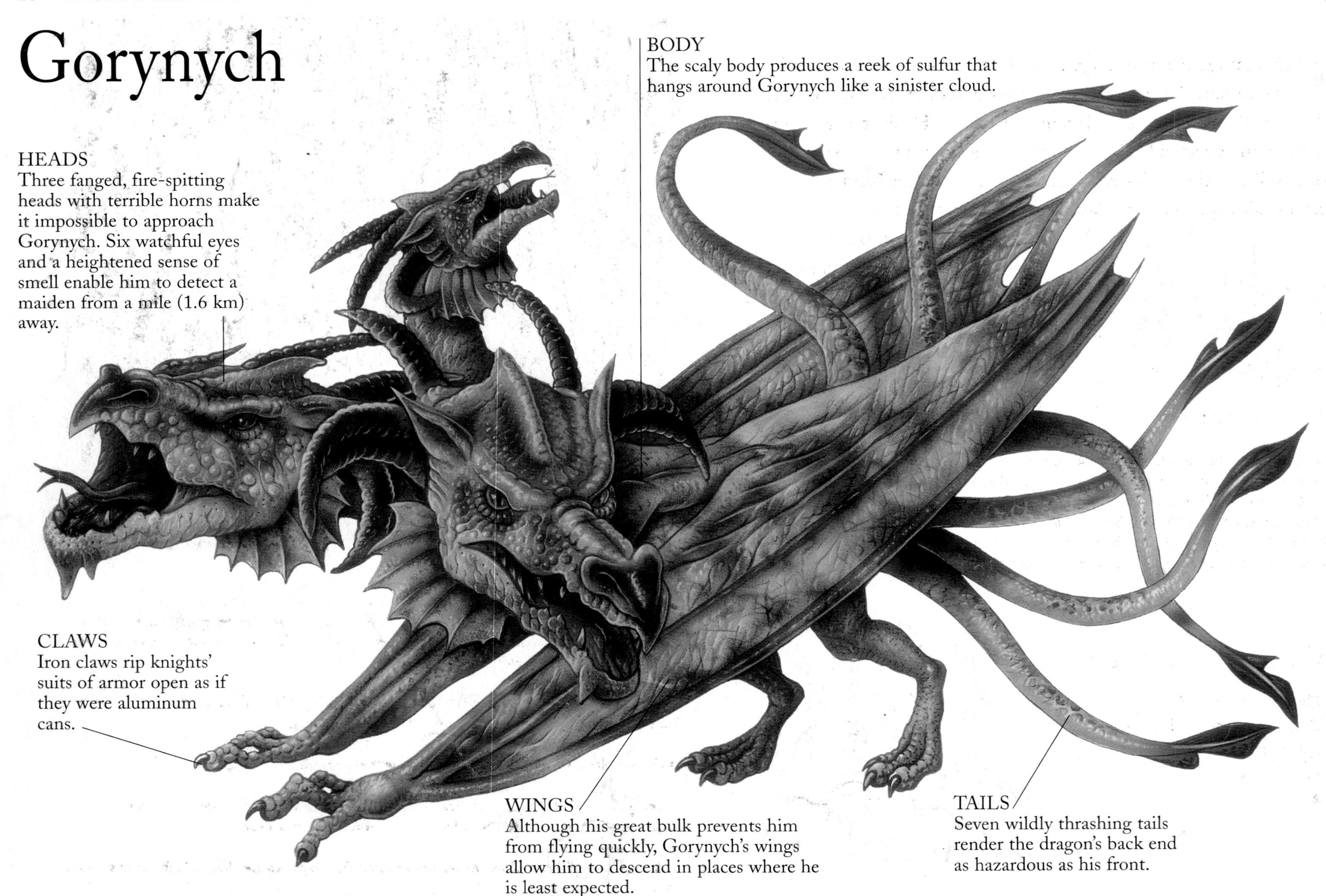
BODY
The scaly body produces a reek of sulfur that hangs around Gorynych like a sinister cloud.
HEADS
Three fanged, fire-spitting heads with terrible horns make it impossible to approach Gorynych. Six watchful eyes and a heightened sense of smell enable him to detect a maiden from a mile (1.6 km) away.
CLAWS
Iron claws rip knights' suits of armor open as if they were aluminum cans.
WINGS
Although his great bulk prevents him from flying quickly, Gorynych's wings allow him to descend in places where he is least expected.
TAILS
Seven wildly thrashing tails render the dragon's back end as hazardous as his front.

This savage Russian dragon has three fire-spitting heads and seven tails. Gorynych walks on his two hind legs and has two small front legs like a Tyrannosaurus rex. His iron claws can slash through any shield or suit of armor. The air around Gorynych reeks of sulfur, a sign of its evil. His uncle, the sorcerer Nemal Chelovek, kidnaps the czar's daughter and intends her to wed Gorynych. The princess is imprisoned in the sorcerer's dark mountain castle. Desperate to have his daughter back, the czar offers a huge reward to anyone who can rescue the princess from the castle. Many princes try and fail.

ACTUAL SIZE

▶ IVAN, A PALACE GUARD who understands the speech of animals, overhears two crows discussing where the princess is hidden. The czar gives Ivan a magic sword to help him on his rescue mission. Nemal Chelovek's fortress is unguarded because he believes no one would dare approach him. Nemal Chelovek turns himself into a giant when he discovers Ivan in his castle. The magic sword flies from Ivan's hands, killing the giant, then flies through the castle halls until it finds and slays Gorynych. Ivan marries the princess.

Where in the world?

The fearsome seven-tailed Gorynych is featured in folktales and myths originating from Russia and Ukraine.

Did you know?

- Gorynych caused eclipses of the Sun and Moon. The fact that they reappeared showed that even a powerful dragon could not defeat the Sun and Moon. The Russians took this as a sign that dragons can be defeated by the righteous.

- Not all Slavic dragons are destructive. The Slovenian city of Ljubljana is protected by a dragon. This benevolent dragon is pictured on the city's coat of arms.

- Dragon blood is so venomous that Earth does not absorb it.

- There are no cave paintings of dragons because caves are a favorite residence of dragons. The dragon residing in the cave would have driven all cave painters away.

- A magic sword that enables the warrior to stand far away from the dragon is the ideal weapon for battle with dragons.

Krak's Dragon

In Polish legend, a fearsome dragon lives in a dark cave at the foot of Wawel Hill along the banks of the Vistula River. Every day it rages through the countryside, terrifying the inhabitants of Krakow. The bad-tempered, fire-breathing dragon eats farm animals and people. Anything that runs from it is fair game. After it gobbles down several small children, it plunders homes for prized possessions to take back to its cave. Many bold knights try to slay this dragon and perish in flame for their efforts. Its daily thefts begin to affect the local economy. The people of the area grow poorer and the princess worries she will never marry.

ACTUAL SIZE

KRAK, A PEASANT BOY employed as a shoemaker's apprentice, is intelligent, cunning, and possessed of unique culinary skills. The king is desperate for anyone's dragon-slaying services and allows the raggedly dressed boy to try. Krak stuffs three roasted sheep full of sulfur and hot spices and leaves the spicy meal next to the dragon's cave. The greedy dragon gulps them down whole. The spices and sulfur burn the dragon's stomach. It drinks half the Vistula River to quench its thirst. Its swollen, burning gut bursts and kills it.

Where in the world?

Every citizen of Poland is familiar with the stories of the death, trauma, and destruction caused by Krak's dragon.

Did you know?

- The city of Krakow is named after the heroic Krak.
- Near the cavern beneath the castle of Krakow, there is a monument to Krak's dragon. The statue of the dragon has been rigged with a natural-gas nozzle so that it breathes fire every few minutes.
- Krak marries the princess and is given the dragon's hoarded treasure. After the death of the king, Krak ascends the throne.
- Many dragons prefer to sleep on top of a pile of jewels and treasure because more traditional bedding materials are too easily ignited by their fiery breath.
- Trickery is often the preferred method for defeating the most dangerous dragons. Cunning is generally a mightier weapon than a sword when facing a beast of such tremendous size, aggression, and appetite.

Knucker

EYES
Eerie eyes glow with a chemical that allows the Knucker to see great distances in the densest waters and on land.

TAIL
Capable of swatting down trees, the gigantic tail is the dragon's most dangerous appendage.

WINGS
Small wings allow the Knucker to fly low through marshy areas in search of likely victims. When in water, the wings act as fins.

JAWS
Immense jaws open wide enough to swallow a horse and cart whole. Teeth larger than railroad spikes line a mouth that reeks of the Knucker's nauseating breath.

BODY
A streamlined, eel-shaped body aids the Knucker in navigating quickly and silently through the chilly waters of the knuckerhole.

A terrible, water-dwelling dragon, the Knucker makes nightly raids on Lyminster farms for meals of horses and cows. Any person crossing its path is just another meal to the Knucker. The dragon squeezes its prey to death or shreds its victim's flesh to ribbons with its poisonous fangs. The thrashing of the Knucker's immense tail topples the trees in Batworth Park. Many a still night in Lyminster is shattered by the hiss and roar of the ravenous dragon. So many villagers and farm animals go missing that the mayor offers a reward to anyone who can kill the Knucker and allow the villagers to live without fear.

ACTUAL SIZE

▶ JIM, A FARMER'S BOY FROM A NEARBY VILLAGE, tells the mayor his plan to defeat the Knucker. The mayor orders the villagers to help Jim with everything he needs. The villagers give Jim all the ingredients for an enormous pie. Jim bakes a gigantic pie laced with poison for the Knucker. He hauls the pie out to the knuckerhole using a borrowed cart and horse. The Knucker eats the pie, horse, and cart. The poison kills the dreaded dragon and Jim chops off its head with an ax.

Where in the world?

The Knucker rises from the knuckerhole in Lyminster, West Sussex. Its residence, the knuckerhole, is a bottomless pool fed by an underground spring.

Did you know?

- St. Mary Magdalene Church in Lyminster contains the Slayer's Slab, a gravestone dedicated to the hero who killed the Knucker.
- The British explorer Sir Francis Drake was called "The Dragon" by the Spanish because he was a fierce warrior and he helped defeat the Spanish Armada.
- The knuckerhole where the Knucker lives is a bottomless pool that neither freezes in winter nor dries up in summer. Six bell ropes from Lyminster Church were tied together and let down in the knuckerhole to measure its depth, but the bottom was never found.
- Residents of Lyminster once used water from the knuckerhole as a cure-all tonic.
- The county of Sussex once had a thriving dragon population. Bignor Hill and St. Leonard's Forest in Sussex also have a history of dragon infestations.

Orochi

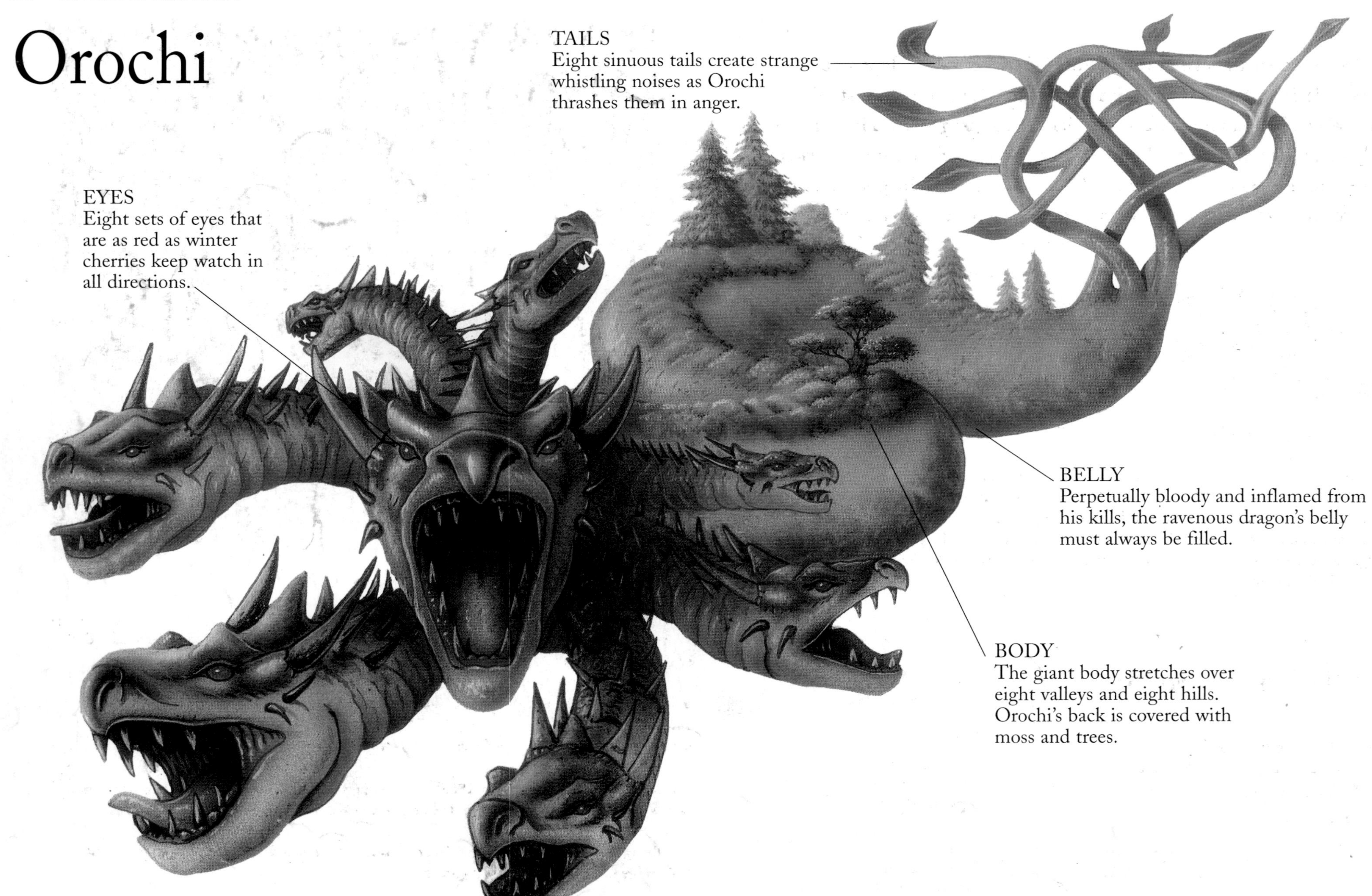
TAILS
Eight sinuous tails create strange whistling noises as Orochi thrashes them in anger.
EYES
Eight sets of eyes that are as red as winter cherries keep watch in all directions.
BELLY
Perpetually bloody and inflamed from his kills, the ravenous dragon's belly must always be filled.
BODY
The giant body stretches over eight valleys and eight hills. Orochi's back is covered with moss and trees.

Each year the evil dragon Orochi demands that a Japanese maiden be offered to him in sacrifice. Even the bravest of warriors cannot defeat this vicious, cunning beast. His gigantic body slithers across eight hills and valleys, and his eight hungry heads make him impossible to approach. One day Susanoo, the god of the sea and storms, comes upon two weeping parents. Seven of their daughters have been devoured by Orochi in the past seven years. Now their eighth and only remaining daughter is to be sacrificed to Orochi. Susanoo agrees to slay the dragon if their eighth daughter will be his wife.

ACTUAL SIZE

▶ SUSANOO TRANSFORMS THE MAIDEN into a comb, which he safely hides in his hair. Susanoo arranges eight enormous vats of rice wine in a circle and leaves them out to tempt the dragon. Attracted by the smell of the strong wine, Orochi plunges each of his eight heads into a vat and drinks greedily. The drunken dragon collapses helpless to the ground and Susanoo uses his powerful sword to slice Orochi to pieces. The local river runs red with the blood of the slain menace.

Where in the world?

Orochi's eight hungry heads terrorized the citizens of Izumo Province in Japan near the foot of Mount Sentsuzan.

JAPAN

Did you know?

- As Susanoo hacks up Orochi, he discovers a sacred sword embedded in one of his tails. The screams of the dying dragon could be heard throughout even the furthest islands of Japan.
- The dragon's full name, Yamata no Orochi, means "big snake of eight branches."
- Fresh maidens are a favorite meal of dragons worldwide.
- During the Edo period (1603-1868), it was popular for Japanese firefighters to get dragon tattoos. They believed the image of the dragon would protect them while fighting fires.
- Although fearsome and powerful, Japanese dragons are also fair and benevolent. The Japanese believe dragons bring wealth and good luck.
- Images of dragons adorn many Buddhist temples in Japan. Dragons are thought to dispel evil.

St. George and the Dragon

TAIL
A flick of this dragon's razor-sharp tail leaves a man with bloodied stumps where he once had limbs.

HEAD
The solid, thick skull contains eyes with extra optic nerves for keen vision and nostrils that belch foul black fumes.

WINGS
Wing bones attached to the broad back by a system of mighty muscles lift the heavy beast into the air.

NECK
An elongated neck keeps the dragon's fire-breathing apparatus at a safe distance from its own body. It also aids in spotting tender maidens and scrappy saints from around corners.

BODY
Scales like steel plates on the dragon's body shatter St. George's spear when he first attempts to stab the creature.

CLAWS
Sturdy talons leave tell-tale gouges in the turf wherever the dragon walks.

This bloodthirsty dragon lives by a spring that provides all the water for the city of Cyrene. Whenever the citizens of Cyrene want water, they are faced with the immense beast. Unhappy with the diet of sheep the citizens feed it, the dragon demands human sacrifices. A human sacrifice has to be given to the dragon daily before it allows anyone to draw water from the spring. The only fair way to determine the daily victim is by drawing lots. The princess is chosen as the next victim and her father, the king, is distraught. He offers the citizens all his riches if they will spare his daughter, but the citizens refuse.

ACTUAL SIZE

▶ THE PRINCESS IS TIED TO A WOODEN STAKE near the spring. St. George, a soldier of the Roman Empire, discovers the distressed princess and unties her. St. George charges the dragon on horseback. His sturdy lance penetrates deep enough only to wound the foul creature. Using the princess's sash as a leash, St. George and the princess lead the injured dragon into town. St. George announces he will finish off the dragon if the citizens convert to Christianity. They agree to convert and St. George draws his sword and kills the dragon.

Where in the world?

This dragon nests at a spring that provides water for the citizens of Cyrene, Libya, which is situated in northern Africa.

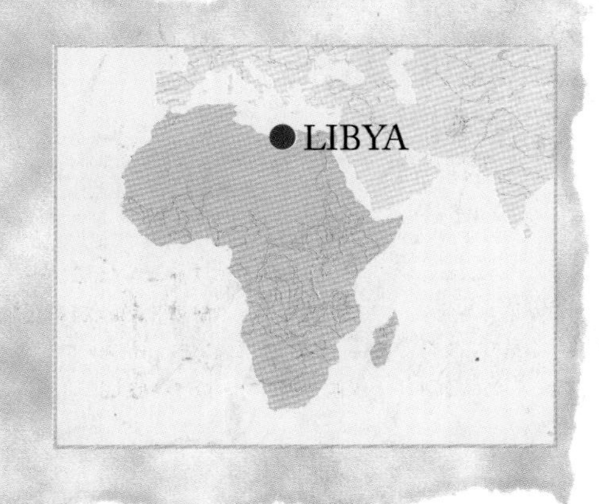

Did you know?

- St. George is the patron saint of England, knights, archers, and butchers.
- The flag of Wales bears the image of a red dragon. It is believed to be the oldest national flag still in use.
- Hundreds of years ago, dinosaur fossils were believed to be dragon bones.
- Dragoon soldiers carried a musket called the dragon. The musket was given this name because it emitted flames when fired.
- The various parts of the dragon are believed to have magical properties. Anyone eating dragon's heart would be able to understand the speech of birds. Eating dragon's tongue gives one the power to win any argument. Dragon's blood provides protection against injury from swords.

Wyvern

TAIL
A pointed tail adds to the wyvern's terrifying appearance and inflicts deep wounds on its prey.
WINGS
The wyvern unfolds its broad wings and flaps them furiously while hissing, creating an effect guaranteed to paralyze its victims with fear.
BODY
Although not the largest of dragons, the wyvern is surprisingly well armored. Its shiny scales fend off most lances and projectiles.
JAWS
Lined with dangerous, flesh-ripping teeth, the wyvern's mouth emits a noxious, poisonous gas that brings about outbreaks of the plague.
CLAWS
Curved talons provide a firm grip on the carcasses that the wyvern flies back to its lair.

The most famous wyvern is one adopted as a pet by young Maud. While walking in the woods near her home in Mordiford, Maud discovers a baby wyvern. Its body is no bigger than a cucumber and is covered in sparkling, bright-green scales. Maud takes the helpless wyvern home, but her parents forbid her to keep it. Instead of setting it free, Maud places the tiny dragon in her secret hiding place in the woods. She visits it daily, feeding it milk and playing with it. The wyvern grows rapidly and soon milk is not enough to satisfy its ravenous appetite. The wyvern begins to feast on local livestock.

ACTUAL SIZE

▶ THE WYVERN QUICKLY DISCOVERS that farmers make better meals than farm animals. Despite its newly acquired taste for human flesh, the wyvern remains gentle with Maud. Garston, a man from one of Mordiford's best families, dons his armor and rides out to slay the wyvern. His sturdy shield protects Garston from the flame-spouting wyvern. Garston pierces the wyvern's shiny scales with his sword, fatally wounding the creature. Maud kneels on the bloodied grass beside the wyvern. Weeping, she cradles her dying friend in her arms.

Where in the world?

In medieval Mordiford, Herefordshire, in England, wyverns were plentiful. It seemed almost anyone could stumble across one with little effort.

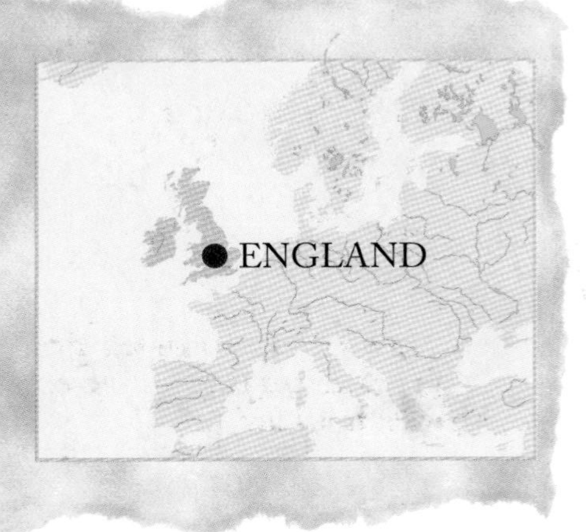

Did you know?

- Because of their flesh-eating habits, wyverns make unsatisfactory pets. Although they are harmless as babies, a dragon's bloodthirsty instincts always set in when it reaches adulthood.
- The wyvern is associated with war, pestilence, and envy. It is believed to bring outbreaks of the plague wherever it goes.
- Its traits of strength, power, and endurance made the wyvern a popular symbol on medieval coats of arms. Its image on shields was used to strike fear into the hearts of enemies.
- British dragons have been known to inhabit places as diverse as caves, fields, woods, swamps, gullies, moors, corn stacks, water holes, and abbey ruins.
- The coat of arms of Moscow bears the image of a soldier on horseback spearing a wyvern.

Apalala

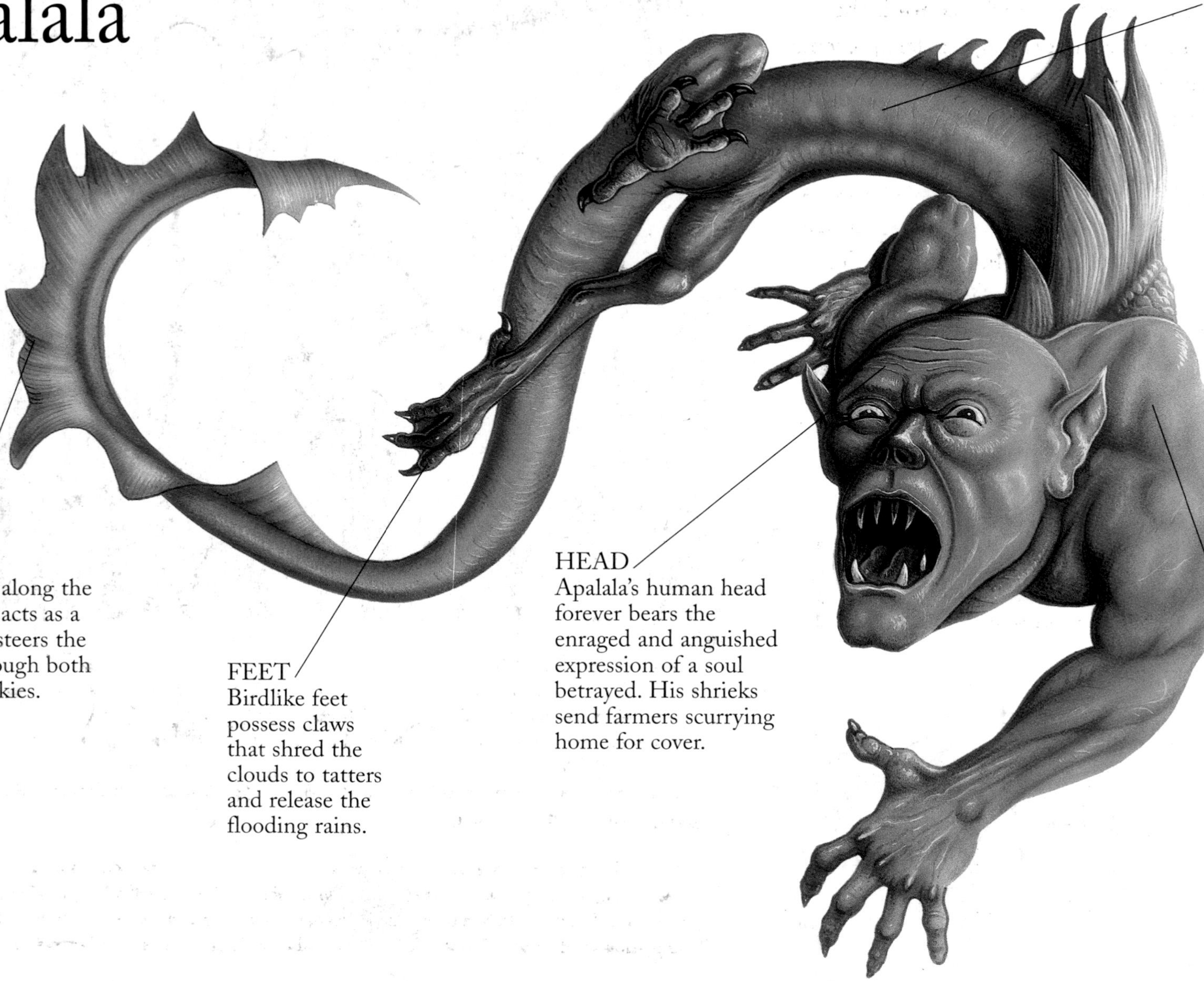

LOWER BODY
By flexing his muscular, serpentine lower body back and forth, the water dragon propels himself through the air and water.

TAIL
A dorsal fin along the dragon's tail acts as a rudder that steers the creature through both waters and skies.

FEET
Birdlike feet possess claws that shred the clouds to tatters and release the flooding rains.

HEAD
Apalala's human head forever bears the enraged and anguished expression of a soul betrayed. His shrieks send farmers scurrying home for cover.

UPPER BODY
The upper half of Apalala's body is human. Although he lacks wings, he is one of the most accomplished of fliers among dragons. When angered he tears through the air just above the ungrateful farmers who neglected his gifts.

Apalala is a powerful naga, a water dragon who controls the rains and rivers. A wise and cunning dragon, Apalala prevents evil dragons from creating violent rain storms and floods. The people of his land are grateful for his protection. Their crops are healthy and abundant. Each year they present Apalala with a tribute of grain to thank him. However, after many years without damaging floods, some of the people stop giving Apalala their yearly tribute of grain. This neglect angers Apalala and he changes into a poisonous dragon. He terrifies the people and destroys all the crops with heavy rains and floods.

ACTUAL SIZE

▶ ONE DAY THE BUDDHA comes to Apalala's land and feels compassion for the people whose crops are being destroyed by the angry dragon. The Buddha speaks with Apalala and convinces him that plaguing the countryside with floods is wrong. Apalala converts to Buddhism and promises not to rage against the countryside any longer. He merely asks that he be given one crop every 12 years. So every 12 years there are heavy rains in the land and Apalala receives the flooded crop as a gift.

Where in the world?

Apalala, the powerful water-dwelling dragon who controls rains and floods, makes his home in the Swat River of Pakistan.

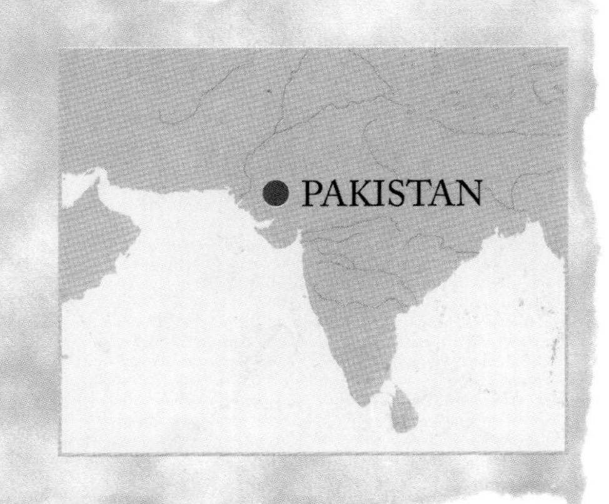

Did you know?

- After his conversion to Buddhism, Apalala created only enough yearly rainfall to ensure the crops would be healthy. The prosperity of all the farmers depends upon the goodwill of Apalala.

- In Kashmir, springs are the main source of water. Numerous temples dedicated to the worship of nagas were built near springs.

- In Buddhism, an animal is not allowed to become a monk. There was once a naga who wanted to be a monk so badly that he changed into human form. When he fell asleep, he changed back into a naga. Buddha told him he could not become a monk and the naga wept bitterly. Out of compassion for the naga, Buddha declared that all candidates for monkhood be called "Naga."

Fafnir

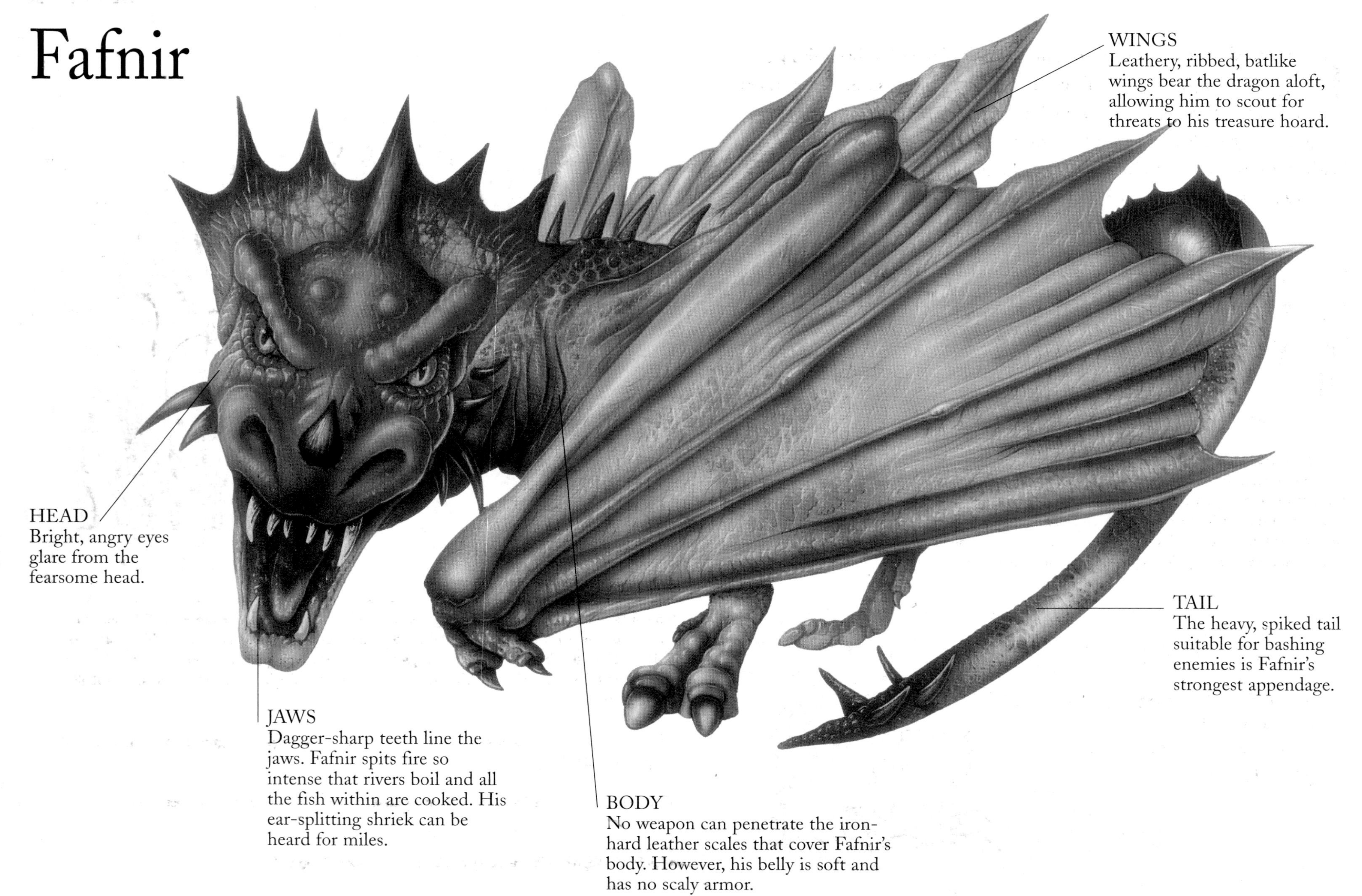
WINGS
Leathery, ribbed, batlike wings bear the dragon aloft, allowing him to scout for threats to his treasure hoard.
HEAD
Bright, angry eyes glare from the fearsome head.
TAIL
The heavy, spiked tail suitable for bashing enemies is Fafnir's strongest appendage.
JAWS
Dagger-sharp teeth line the jaws. Fafnir spits fire so intense that rivers boil and all the fish within are cooked. His ear-splitting shriek can be heard for miles.
BODY
No weapon can penetrate the iron-hard leather scales that cover Fafnir's body. However, his belly is soft and has no scaly armor.

Greed gave rise to this mighty dragon. One of a dwarf-king's three ogre sons, Fafnir covets his father's treasure. He murders his father and transforms himself into a fearsome, wicked dragon who guards all the gold. Fafnir's dragon body is covered with leather scales that are as hard as iron. No known weapon can penetrate his hide. His ridged spine ends in a spiked tail that he uses to thrash anyone who comes near his lair. He is able to boil rivers with his fiery breath until all the fish within it are cooked. Greed runs in Fafnir's family. His brother Regin covets the treasure that Fafnir stole from their father.

ACTUAL SIZE

▶ REGIN PERSUADES BRAVE SIGURD TO SLAY THE DRAGON. Once Fafnir is dead, Regin plans to steal the treasure and kill Sigurd. Sigurd knows he cannot defeat Fafnir with brute force, so he digs a trench along the path the dragon takes. Armed with his father's sword, Sigurd hides in the trench, pulling branches and leaves over the opening so the dragon will not see him. Sigurd waits until Fafnir passes overhead and thrusts his sword into the dragon's soft belly. Fafnir dies in agony from the fatal wound.

Where in the world?

A figure from Norse mythology, Fafnir is known in the Scandinavian countries of Sweden, Denmark, and Norway.

Did you know?

- Sigurd's hands are wet with the dragon's blood after the slaying. He removes Fafnir's heart to roast it on a fire so Regin can eat it. When Sigurd wipes his bloodied hand across his mouth, he accidentally tastes Fafnir's blood. The magical properties of dragon blood allow him to understand the speech of birds. The birds warn Sigurd that Regin plans to kill him and steal all the treasure.

- Regin brews a poisoned broth that he intends to use to kill Sigurd. Sigurd forces Regin to drink the poison instead.

- Keen eyesight allows Fafnir to spot the glint of a precious jewel from great distances, even in dim light.

- Richard Wagner tells the story of Fafnir in his opera *Siegfried*.

Futs-Lung

BODY
Futs-Lung can transform himself into any shape he desires or make himself completely invisible. He creates new hills when he hunches his back underground.
FIN
The scalloped dorsal fin along the length of his back stabilizes the dragon as he maneuvers through the air, water, and earth at lightning-fast speeds.
EYES
The dragon's bulging eyes can see into the depths of the earth where his treasure is stored.
CHIN
Hidden beneath his chin is the pearl of wisdom. The pearl glows from within and is a vessel of health.
JAWS
Futs-Lung's voice is like the jingling of copper pans, banging gongs, or ringing bells, depending upon his mood. His furious roar brings forth earthquakes.

The dragon of hidden treasures that lives deep within the Earth is Futs-Lung. He guards all the precious gems and priceless metals in his lair. Futs-Lung possesses a magic pearl that multiplies when touched. Since the pearl represents wisdom, it is considered the most valuable of all his treasures. It takes 3,000 years for Futs-Lung to grow to his terrific adult size. Newly hatched, he looks much like an eel. By 500 years of age, Futs-Lung has grown a head that resembles a carp's. By his $1{,}500^{th}$ birthday, he will grow a long tail, a head with a thick beard, and four stumpy legs with claws. At the age of 2,000, Futs-Lung will have horns.

ACTUAL SIZE

▶ In modern-day Hong Kong there is an apartment complex that was built near a mountain where Futs-Lung lives. The complex was designed with a large gap in the middle so that Futs-Lung's ocean view would remain unobstructed and his goodwill would be maintained. Like most Chinese dragons, Futs-Lung is benevolent until offended. His wrath should not be roused. He must be treated with respect and reverence so he does not unleash his incredible temper. Volcanoes are formed when Futs-Lung bursts from the earth and reports to heaven.

Where in the world?

Futs-Lung is the underworld dragon of China. He is in charge of guarding all the precious metals and gems buried in earth.

Did you know?

- Imperial Chinese dragons have five toes, Korean dragons four, and Japanese dragons three.
- Chinese dragons lay one egg at a time. Each dragon egg takes 1,000 years to hatch.
- The Chinese refer to themselves as "descendants of the dragon."
- Chinese dragons have 117 scales on their serpentine bodies.
- It was a compliment to refer to someone as "dragon face" in China. Many founding emperors of dynasties were described as having dragon faces. It was considered a lucky sign indicating their future greatness.
- Chinese dragons are shape-shifters that can change into the form of a man, shrink themselves down to a mouse, or expand until they fill up the space between heaven and Earth.

Hatuibwari

HEAD
Four eyes indicate Hatuibwari is wise and all-seeing.

WINGS
Hatuibwari's wings carry him back and forth between the sky and the mountaintops where he lives. Since he has no legs, strong wings are necessary to allow him to hover.

HANDS
The great, clawed hands carefully shaped the first man and woman in Melanesia from clay.

BODY
The serpentine shape of Hatuibwari's torso cuts down on wind resistance and is perfect for darting through the sky. It is also an advantageous design for swimming rapidly through seas.

On San Cristobal Island in Melanesia, the ancient belief is that the dragon Hatuibwari created and nourished all living things. He is the male version of Mother Earth, with a body that is half-human and half-snake. Two enormous wings carry him through the skies and four eyes allow him to see everything under the Sun. Hatuibwari rolls red clay in his hands, breathes on it, and forms the shape of a human. He places the clay figure in the Sun and it comes to life as the first woman. Later, while the first woman is asleep, Hatuibwari takes a rib from her side, adds more clay, and creates the first man.

ACTUAL SIZE

▶ ONE DAY HATUIBWARI coils around his human grandson to comfort him. The child's father comes home and mistakes Hatuibwari for an enormous serpent squeezing the life from his child. The frightened father does not recognize the dragon spirit as his father-in-law and cuts Hatuibwari to pieces with a knife. The pieces unite again at once. Angry and offended, Hatuibwari announces that he is leaving and will cause the people's crops to fail. Hatuibwari departs to live on Guadalcanal Island and everything deteriorates in his absence.

Where in the world?

The Hatuibwari lives in the sky and on sacred mountaintops of San Cristobal and Guadalcanal in the Solomon Islands, Melanesia.

Did you know?

- The Hatuibwari often appears in a sacred grove. Anyone who does not treat the grove with proper reverence and respect is stricken with illness and terrible sores.
- Sacrifices of pigs are offered to Hatuibwari to appease him. Like Chinese and Japanese dragons, he must be treated with respect or he will grow angry.
- Hatuibwari causes rains to fall in order to quench his thirst.
- Babylonian, Chinese, Australian, and Aztec mythologies all contain stories of dragons as creators of life on Earth.
- In Melanesian mythology, Darkness, Forever, and the Sea have always existed. Hatuibwari created animals, food, trees, and humans. He travels between our world and the sky.

Jawzahr

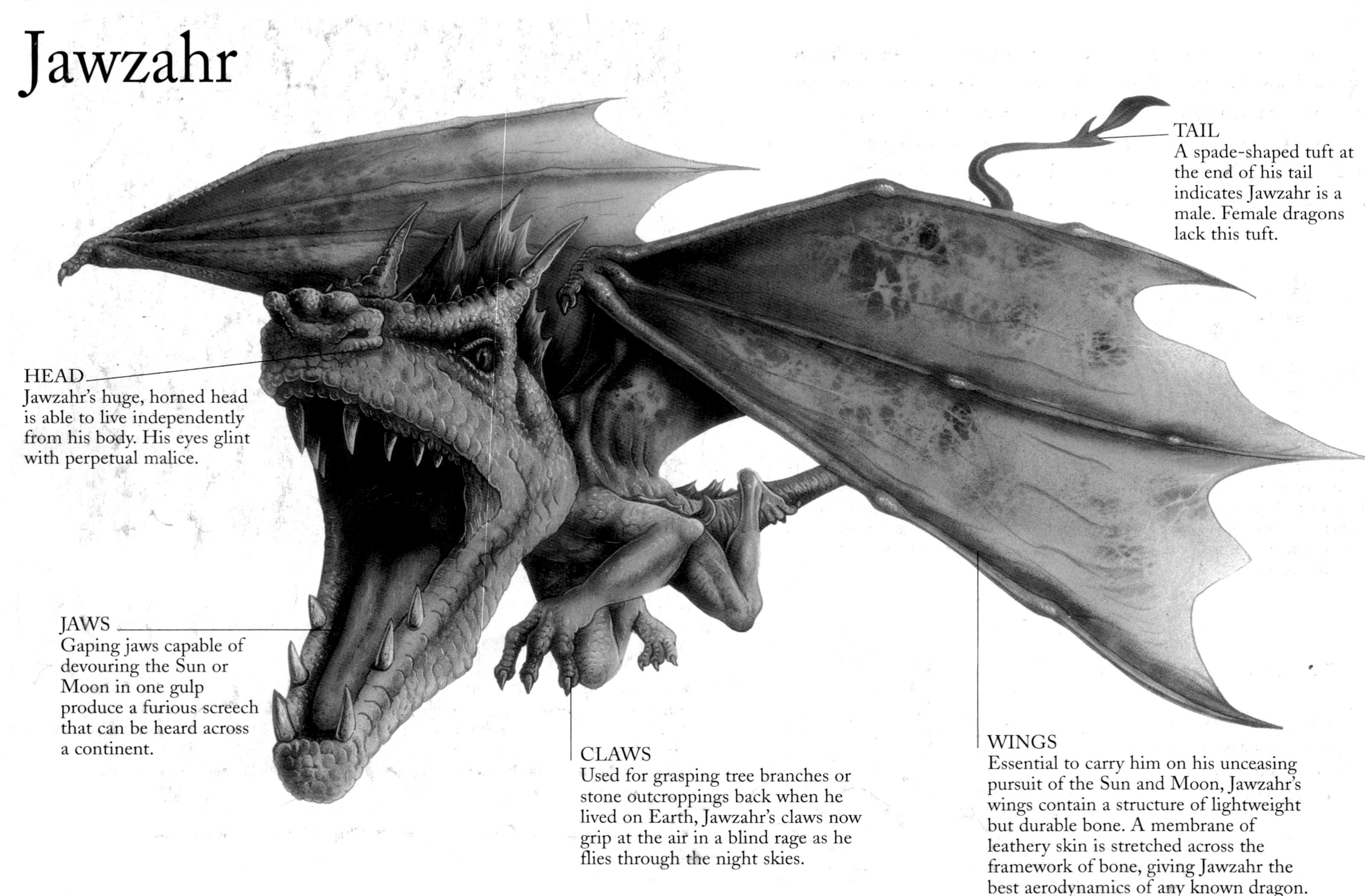
TAIL
A spade-shaped tuft at the end of his tail indicates Jawzahr is a male. Female dragons lack this tuft.
HEAD
Jawzahr's huge, horned head is able to live independently from his body. His eyes glint with perpetual malice.
JAWS
Gaping jaws capable of devouring the Sun or Moon in one gulp produce a furious screech that can be heard across a continent.
CLAWS
Used for grasping tree branches or stone outcroppings back when he lived on Earth, Jawzahr's claws now grip at the air in a blind rage as he flies through the night skies.
WINGS
Essential to carry him on his unceasing pursuit of the Sun and Moon, Jawzahr's wings contain a structure of lightweight but durable bone. A membrane of leathery skin is stretched across the framework of bone, giving Jawzahr the best aerodynamics of any known dragon.

In ancient Persia, eclipses occur when Jawzahr the comet dragon swallows the Sun or Moon. He menaces the two great luminaries, chasing them around the sky and devouring them at regular intervals. Jawzahr commands a legion of demons and is a crafty, curious dragon. He disguises himself as a god one day and drinks an immortality-giving potion meant only for the gods. The Sun and Moon, however, see everything and they report Jawzahr's trickery to the gods. As punishment, Jawzahr's head is severed with one well aimed throw of a discus. But Jawzahr is already immortal because of the potion he drank, and cannot be killed.

ACTUAL SIZE

▶ ENRAGED, JAWZAHR ASCENDS TO THE SKY. The two immortal parts of him live on separate from each other. Jawzahr is angry at both the Sun and Moon for revealing his deception to the gods. He forever chases the Sun and Moon, gobbling them down when he catches them. Any time an eclipse occurs, it means that Jawzahr has caught up with and consumed the Sun or the Moon. As for his tail, it emits a shower of comets that stream across the night sky.

Where in the world?

A dragon from Islamic mythology, Jawzahr first made his appearance in legends from Persia, which is modern-day Iran.

Did you know?

- The astronomical location of the dragon's head and dragon's tail mark the points where solar and lunar eclipses may occur.

- Draco, a constellation in the northern hemisphere, gets its name from the Latin word for dragon. One of the brightest stars in Draco is in its tail and is named Thuban, which is the Arabic word for dragon. Another star in Draco is Rastaban, which means "head of the dragon." About 5,000 years ago Thuban was the Pole Star, Earth's North Star. The ancient Egyptians recognized Thuban as the North Star at the time they were constructing the Great Pyramid. Today our North Star is Polaris.

- Many ancient cultures believed that comets were dragons streaking across the sky.

Ladon

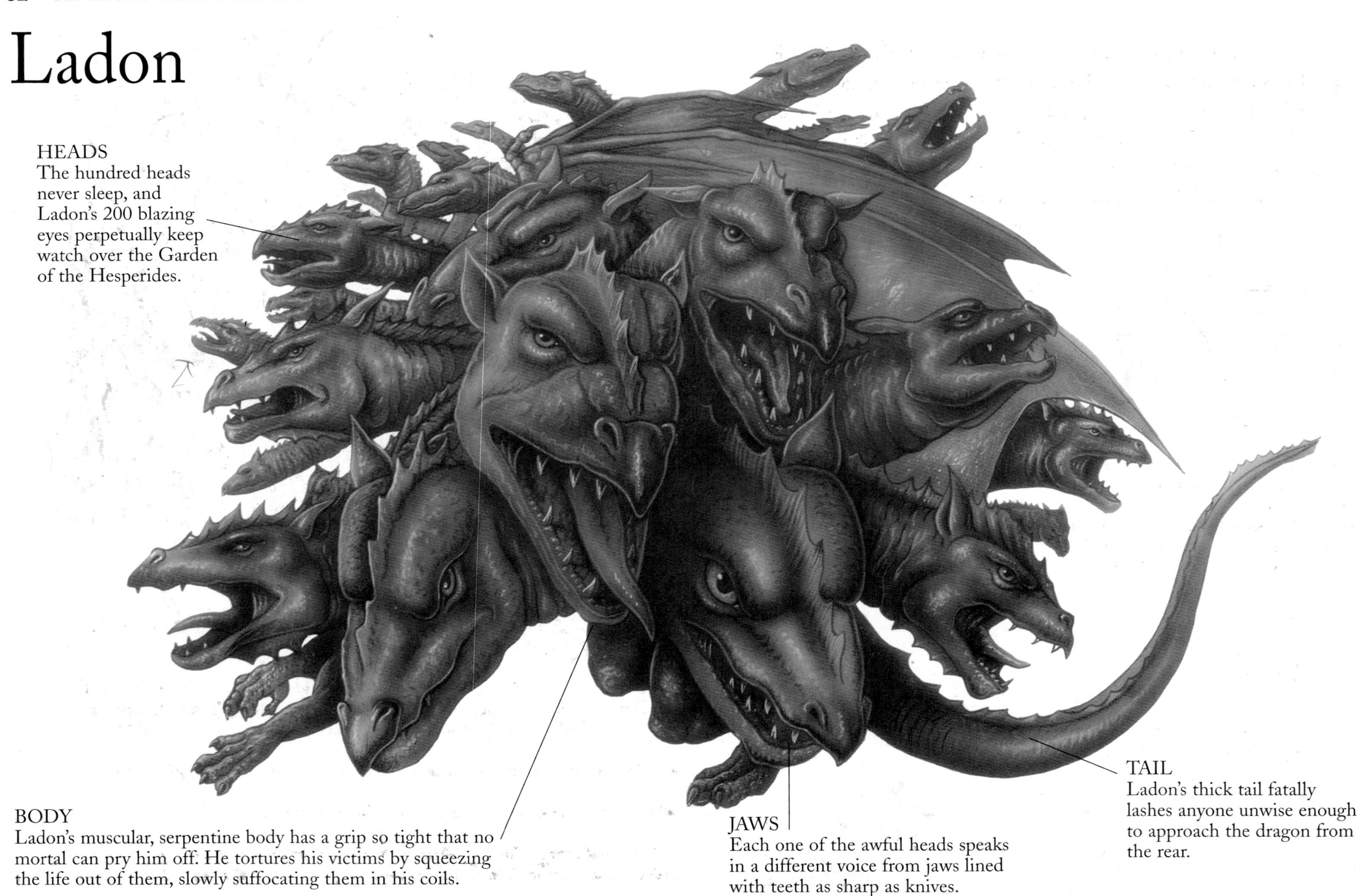
HEADS
The hundred heads never sleep, and Ladon's 200 blazing eyes perpetually keep watch over the Garden of the Hesperides.
BODY
Ladon's muscular, serpentine body has a grip so tight that no mortal can pry him off. He tortures his victims by squeezing the life out of them, slowly suffocating them in his coils.
JAWS
Each one of the awful heads speaks in a different voice from jaws lined with teeth as sharp as knives.
TAIL
Ladon's thick tail fatally lashes anyone unwise enough to approach the dragon from the rear.

In Greek mythology there is a monstrous dragon with 100 heads who twines his serpentine body around a tree bearing golden apples. This beast is Ladon, and he was placed in the Garden of the Hesperides by Hera, queen of the Olympians. His task is to guard the garden and its golden apples. Not one of Ladon's hundred heads ever sleeps and each head speaks with a different voice. Ladon's 200 fiery, watchful eyes ensure that no one approaches the golden apples. Anyone who dares to sail to the ends of the earth in search of Hera's golden apples risks being torn to pieces by Ladon's gigantic teeth or squeezed to death in the coils of his muscular body.

ACTUAL SIZE

▶ THE KING OF MYCENAE TESTS HERACLES by assigning him twelve labors. The eleventh labor requires Heracles to steal the golden apples that Ladon guards. Heracles dips his arrow tips in the gall of a hydra and fires the poisoned arrows over the garden wall at Ladon. The awful dragon is felled by the poisoned arrows and Heracles enters the garden safely. He steals the apples and completes his eleventh labor. Passing sailors later report having seen the slain Ladon with only the tip of his tail still twitching.

Where in the world?

The Garden of the Hesperides, where Ladon winds around the tree of golden apples, lies in the Canary Islands off the coast of Africa, not far from Mount Atlas.

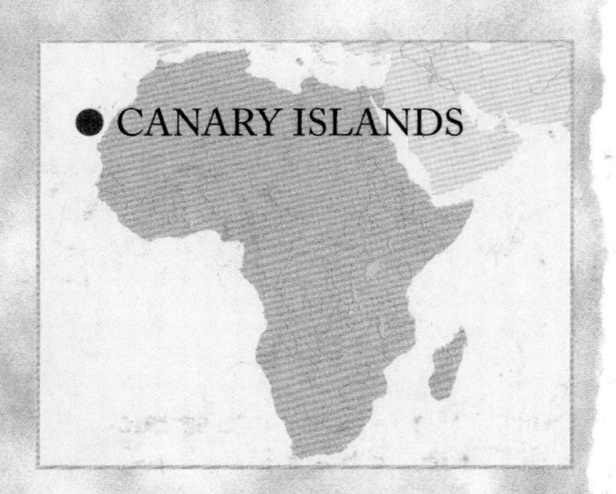

Did you know?

- After his death, Hera places Ladon in the sky as the constellation Draco, where he snakes around the North Pole eternally.
- Where blood from Ladon's wounds drenched the ground, dragon trees sprouted from each drop. Dragon trees have massive trunks and twisted branches. Their sap, called "dragon tree blood," is dark red and is believed to have healing properties.
- In Roman mythology, Heracles is known as Hercules and Hera is called Juno.
- The Latin word for a dragon, "draco," means snake or serpent.
- Direct frontal attack is the least effective way to slay a dragon. Heracles is wise enough to maintain a safe distance from the beast and use the stout garden wall as a shield.

Ryujin

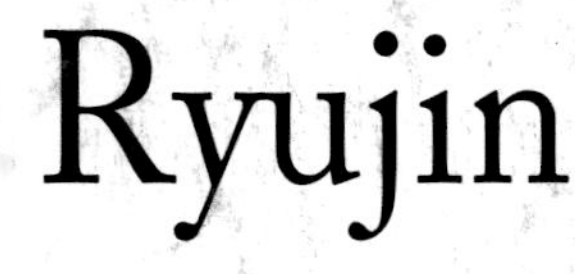

TAIL
A single thrash of Ryujin's tail creates massive tidal waves that wipe out entire coastal villages.

HEAD
His noble head bears the horns of a stag, whiskers that indicate his wisdom, and eyes that see everything from the very bottom of the ocean.

BODY
Ryujin winds his massive, scaly body through the chambers of his underwater palace far beyond the reach of any fisherman or scientist seeking him.

CLAWS
Floods result when Ryujin rakes his impressive claws through the ocean. A swipe of his foot is capable of capsizing an entire fleet of ships.

JAWS
When Ryujin opens his enormous, toothy jaws and inhales, giant whirlpools appear in the water.

In Japanese mythology, Ryujin is the dragon god of the sea. He lives beneath the ocean in a jeweled palace made of red and white coral. His palace has a snowy winter hall, a spring hall where cherry trees grow, a summer hall with chirping crickets, and a fall hall with colorful maple trees. For a human, one day at Ryujin's underwater palace is equal to a hundred years on Earth. Sea turtles, fish, and jellyfish act as the dragon god's loyal servants. Ryujin controls the tides with magical sea jewels. Humans must approach Ryujin carefully because no mortal can glimpse his entire body and survive the sight. When angry, Ryujin churns the waves, causing rough waters for sailors.

ACTUAL SIZE

▶ THE EMPRESS JINGO asks Ryujin for assistance in the attack she plans against Korea. Ryujin's messenger brings her the two tide jewels. Jingo sails toward Korea with the Japanese fleet. The Korean fleet meets them at sea. Jingo flings the low-tide jewel into the sea and all the waters disappear, stranding the Korean ships. When the Korean soldiers leap from their ships to attack on foot, Jingo casts the high-tide jewel onto the seabed. All the waters rush back, drowning the Korean soldiers.

Where in the world?

Ryujin, the dragon god of the sea, lives at the bottom of the ocean near the Ryukyu Islands off the coast of Japan.

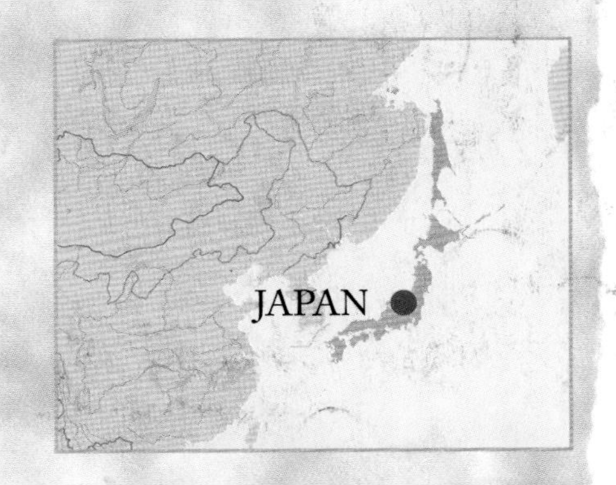

Did you know?

- Ryujin's beautiful daughter married Prince Hoori. This makes Ryujin the ancestor of all the Japanese emperors.

- Because Japanese dragons are related to royalty, no one is allowed to harm them. Since they have nothing to fear from humans, Japanese dragons have become tame over the years. Dragons may be seen blocking traffic in cities or sunning themselves on rocks off Japan's shores.

- Many dragons are shape-shifters. They can change into the form of a human, mate, and produce human offspring.

- In both Japan and China, the dragon is one of the guardian animals of the four directions. The dragon guards the eastern compass point and is associated with the season of spring.

Shen-Lung

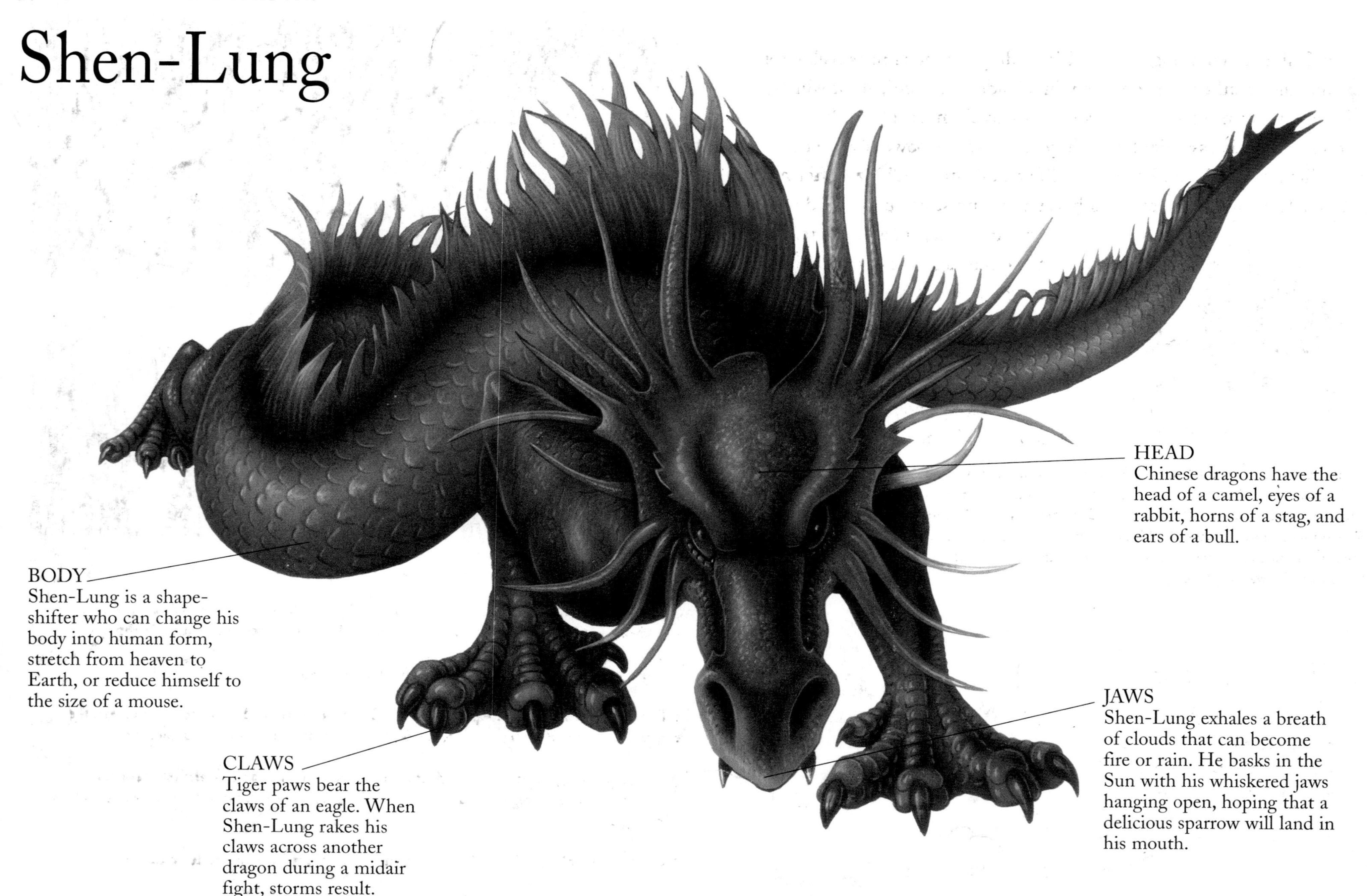
HEAD
Chinese dragons have the head of a camel, eyes of a rabbit, horns of a stag, and ears of a bull.
BODY
Shen-Lung is a shape-shifter who can change his body into human form, stretch from heaven to Earth, or reduce himself to the size of a mouse.
CLAWS
Tiger paws bear the claws of an eagle. When Shen-Lung rakes his claws across another dragon during a midair fight, storms result.
JAWS
Shen-Lung exhales a breath of clouds that can become fire or rain. He basks in the Sun with his whiskered jaws hanging open, hoping that a delicious sparrow will land in his mouth.

In China, Shen-Lung is the spiritual dragon who is responsible for making weather. He controls rain, clouds, and wind, all of which are important in a country with so many farmers. The right amount of rain is essential for healthy crops, so his power over rain gives Shen-Lung the authority over life and death in China. Offerings to Shen-Lung assure a bountiful harvest. He must be approached with the utmost respect and reverence. It is important not to offend Shen-Lung because if he feels neglected his anger is aroused. The result of his wrath is terrible weather in the form of floods or drought, which could destroy the life-giving crops upon which the Chinese depend.

ACTUAL SIZE

▶ BECAUSE OF HIS GREAT POWER, Shen-Lung grows lazy over the years. He shrinks himself to the size of a mouse in order to hide and avoid work. When lightning strikes a house or tree, it is because the thunder god is sending his servant to search for Shen-Lung. Shen-Lung floats across the sky, his body stretching farther than the eye can see. He is benevolent but bad-tempered. The worst floods in Chinese history were unleashed by Shen-Lung when he was offended by a mortal.

Where in the world?

Shen-Lung is the spiritual dragon who has control over the winds and the rains that affect all the crops grown in China.

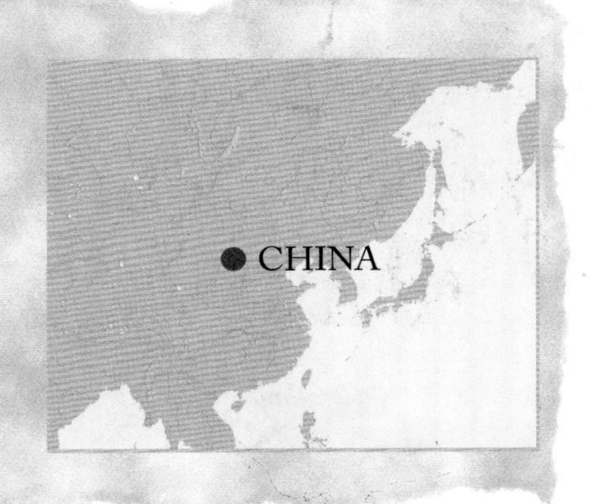

Did you know?

- Shen-Lung's voice is heard in hurricanes and his claws can be seen in flashes of lightning.
- When Shen-Lung is sick, the rain has a distinctly fishy smell.
- The dragon is the emblem representing the Chinese emperor and the phoenix represents the empress. Together, the dragon and the phoenix are used as symbols of marital harmony.
- All Chinese dragons have nine distinct features: the head of a camel, scales of a carp, horns of a stag, eyes of a rabbit, ears of a bull, neck of a snake, belly of a clam, paws of a tiger, and the claws of an eagle.
- The dragon ranks first in the Chinese mythological hierarchy of 360 scaled creatures.
- Glass was thought to be solidified dragon breath.

Glaurung

TAIL
Glaurung's whiplike tail is a deadly weapon. A blow dealt by Glaurung's tail can crumble stone walls or snap a grown man's spine.
BODY
A glimmer of fire shows around the edges of his golden, armorlike scales when Glaurung is enraged. His scales fade to a dull gray when his fury dies down. Only the dragon's slimy belly, which lacks scales, is vulnerable to attack.
EYES
Lidless, unblinking eyes cast a bewitching spell that renders his victims helpless. Everything Glaurung sees is telepathically transmitted to his evil master, Morgoth.
JAWS
Flames as hot as lava shoot from Glaurung's jaws, scorching everything within 40 feet of the beast. When not spouting fire, his breath has the distinctly putrid reek of decaying animal flesh.

Glaurung the Deceiver, or the Worm of Greed, is the Father of Dragons. Bred by Morgoth the Enemy, Glaurung uses trickery and deception to spread lies. He enjoys creating misery and confusion in others. The dragon wreaks as much havoc using the spells he casts as he does on the battlefield using brute force. Glaurung is corrupt and foul-smelling, able to taint pure waters with his mere presence. He serves as the eyes of evil Morgoth, who senses everything the dragon sees. Before he is fully mature, Glaurung participates in battle, but his armor is not fully hardened and cannot withstand the archers' arrows.

ACTUAL SIZE

▶ GLAURUNG CASTS DRAGON SPELLS with his lidless, unblinking eyes. He fills the head of the heroic Túrin with lies and self-doubt. Túrin's sister, Nienor, is also victim of Glaurung's spell. She is spellbound with complete forgetfulness and cannot remember her own name. As a result, Nienor unwittingly marries her brother. In order to slay the deceiver, Túrin clings to a cliffside above a deep gorge where Glaurung passes. When the dragon slithers overhead, Túrin kills Glaurung by thrusting his black sword into the beast's soft belly.

Where in the world?

Glaurung is the first and fiercest of the land-dwelling fire drakes of J.R.R. Tolkien's Middle Earth in *The Silmarillion*. Glaurung builds a nest upon the treasure in the tunnels beneath Nargothrond after the city is sacked.

Did you know?

- When Glaurung dies, both Túrin and Nienor are released from the dragon's spell. Both commit suicide when they discover they have married a sibling.
- Blood issues from the fatal wound when Túrin pulls the black sword from Glaurung's body. The poisonous blood burns Túrin's hand
- Glaurung, red-hot with wrath, lies in a river where he generates a horrible reek and foul vapors that blind people until they lose their way. Even horses are driven mad by the dragon's stench.
- Anyone foolish enough to look Glaurung directly in the eye is immediately rendered helpless by his dragon spell.
- Glaurung led the assault in the Battle of Sudden Flame, but was knifed in the belly and had to flee the battlefield to heal.

Hungarian Horntail

HEAD
The terrible head bears bronze horns used to gore its victims. Its hearing is so acute that the dragon can detect any approaching threat from a great distance away.

TAIL
A whip of the spike-lined tail easily deals a mortal blow to the dragon's enemies. When angered, the thrashing tail rips up large patches of sod.

EYES
The yellow eyes with vertical pupils contain a reflective layer that enables the dragon to detect things five times more effectively than a human can.

CLAWS
Sharp, curved claws slash at the flesh of enemies or grip its victim's body as the dragon's fangs carry out their gruesome work.

JAWS
When not producing a yowling, screeching scream that curdles the blood, the jaws emit a stream of fire that reaches as far as 50 feet (15 m).

As the first task of the Triwizard Tournament in J.K. Rowling's *Harry Potter and the Goblet of Fire*, Harry must get past a mother Hungarian Horntail and steal a golden egg from her nest. The golden egg is placed among her clutch of gray eggs. A nesting mother Horntail is especially hazardous when defending her young. Harry summons his racing broom and uses it to fly back and forth, taunting the dragon. He dodges blasts of fire deftly on his broom, but has one shoulder scraped by her thrashing, spiked tail. He lures the furious dragon up onto her hind legs by flying high above her, then swoops down and snatches the golden egg.

ACTUAL SIZE

▶ THE HUNGARIAN HORNTAIL IS REMARKABLY DANGEROUS because it can do as much damage with its spike-lined tail as it can with its fanged mouth, which shoots jets of fire up to a distance of 50 feet (15 m). The young use their spiked tails to club their way out of their eggs. It can require anywhere from six to eight well-trained wizards to subdue a fully grown Hungarian Horntail with stunning spells. It is considered the most dangerous of all dragon breeds, according to the Ministry of Magic.

Where in the world?

Normally native to Hungary, smuggling of the Hungarian Horntail's eggs has led to sightings of the dragon in England.

Did you know?

- The blood, heart, horn, hide, and liver of dragons all have magical properties.
- There are 10 breeds of purebred dragon that can interbreed and produce hybrid dragons.
- The female dragon is larger and more aggressive than the male dragon.
- The motto for Hogwarts School of Witchcraft and Wizardry—*Draco Dormiens Nunquam Titillandus*—means "Never tickle a sleeping dragon."
- The dinosaur *Dracorex Hogwartsia*, which means "dragon king of Hogwarts," was named by young visitors to the Children's Museum of Indianapolis.
- The Ministry of Magic has classified the Hungarian Horntail as a known wizard-killer.

Luckdragon

BACK
Falkor's enormous back accommodates heroes who need to be carried through the air on important quests.

EYES
Eyes glow in the luckdragon's noble head. He is able to spot landmarks far below him on the ground even when traveling through the clouds at top speed.

JAWS
Falkor's lionlike mouth produces blue flame. The luckdragon is the only dragon known to spew blue fire. His song sounds like the golden note of a large bell.

BODY
The long, graceful body with pearl-colored scales requires no wings for soaring. The luckdragon uses levitation for flight rather than traditional dragon wings.

A dragon species in Michael Ende's novel *The Neverending Story*, the luckdragon is a wingless beast that flies by levitating. Falkor, the luckdragon in the novel, is unlike the traditional terrifying dragon. He is an optimist, believing in the power of good luck and perseverance. He tells young Atreyu that if he never gives up, good luck will find him. Even when Falkor is trapped in an enormous web stretched across Deep Chasm and struggling against a swarm of poisonous insects, he does not give up. Falkor credits Atreyu with helping him escape the web. He carries the boy on his back in search of the Southern Oracle.

ACTUAL SIZE

▶ FALKOR IS AS TALENTED AS HE IS KIND. Despite his enormous size, he is as light as a summer cloud and needs no wings to fly. He can fly while sleeping, fly on his back, and perform perfect loop-the-loops. Falkor whizzes through the mists and shreds of clouds so rapidly that Atreyu gasps for breath. When circling the night sky above the Lake of Tears, Falkor sings a song of pure joy in his bell-like voice, which is so beautiful it opens the heart of every listener.

Where in the world?

Falkor the luckdragon lives in the land of Fantastica, a place where the geography is ever-changing because it is determined by wishes.

Did you know?

- Luckdragons feed on air and heat. They require no other food. Without air and heat they live only a short time.
- Viewed from the earth, a luckdragon flying overhead resembles a slow flash of lightning or a white flame.
- The rider traveling on the back of a luckdragon experiences a smooth ride despite the great speed of travel.
- As a creature of air and fire, water is the luckdragon's enemy. Water can suffocate or extinguish the flame of a luckdragon because they are always inhaling air.
- Falkor understands the language of water because all the languages of joy are closely related.

Norwegian Ridgeback

Hagrid, keeper of the keys and grounds at Hogwarts, keeps a baby Norwegian Ridgeback named Norbert as a pet in J.K. Rowling's *Harry Potter and the Sorcerer's Stone*. Hagrid wins the black dragon egg from a stranger during a card game and secretly brings it back to Hogwarts. He hatches the egg by placing it in the center of a fire. Within one week Norbert is three times his original size and smoke is issuing from his nostrils. Norbert sneezes sparks, a sign he will soon develop into a full-fledged fire-breather. The Norwegian Ridgeback can breathe fire at one to three months old, earlier than any other breed.

ACTUAL SIZE

▶ ACCORDING TO *Fantastic Beasts and Where to Find Them* by Newt Scamander, a required text at Hogwarts School, the Norwegian Ridgeback is extremely aggressive to its own kind, making it a rare dragon. Legend states that one carried away and devoured a baby whale off the coast of Norway in 1802. Norbert is a hazard in captivity. His tail banging against the wall rattles windows and wounds from the bite of his poisonous fangs turn green. Hagrid must feed Norbert dead rats by the crate to satisfy his ravenous appetite.

Where in the world?

The Norwegian Ridgeback originated in the Norwegian mountains, where it eats water-dwelling creatures and singes the landscape on a regular basis. There have also been sightings at Hogwarts in England and in Romania.

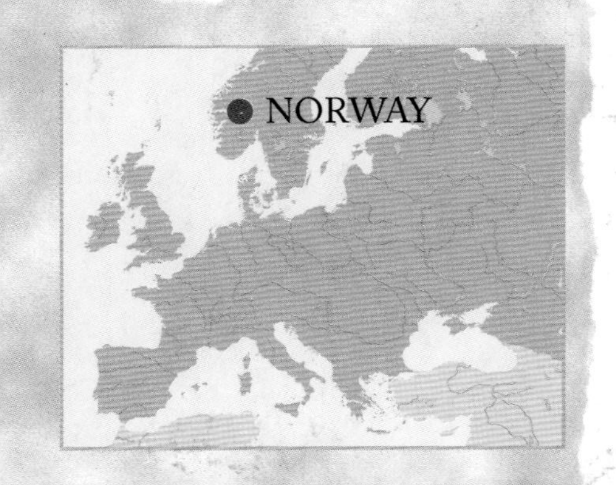

Did you know?

- According to Headmaster Dumbledore, one of the 12 uses of dragon's blood is as oven cleaner.
- The Warlock's Convention of 1709 outlawed dragon breeding. It is illegal to keep a dragon as a pet in the wizarding world.
- Dragon eggs are considered Class A Non-Tradable Goods.
- Hatchlings should be fed a bucket of chicken-blood-and-brandy mixture.
- Despite Hagrid's good intentions, Norwegian Ridgebacks are impossible to train or domesticate.
- It is especially unwise to keep a fire-breathing dragon as a pet if you live in a wooden house.

Smaug

EYES
Blazing eyes emit a thin, piercing red beam that casts a dragon spell.
WINGS
A noise like a roaring wind is produced by the flapping of Smaug's enormous wings.
JAWS
Smaug's fiery breath at full force reduces every building in town to a heap of ashes. He produces a roar that is so fierce and deafening it causes avalanches.
LEGS
Muscular legs trample the ground with power enough to shake the roots of mountains. His claws are capable of crushing boulders.
TAIL
A single sweep of Smaug's mighty tail is all it takes to smash the roof of Esgaroth's Great House.
BODY
Nothing, not a sword nor arrow nor curse, can penetrate Smaug's tough hide. However, there is one spot on his underside that is vulnerable.

Isolated deep within the Lonely Mountain, Smaug the Golden sleeps atop the pile of treasure that he stole from the dwarves. Smaug makes his bed on the mass of ornaments, utensils, weapons, and gems that he hoards. He lies upon the gems for so long that they stick to his soft belly, forming a dazzling protective armor. At the end of a hot tunnel in a dungeon hall dug by dwarves, Smaug's gurgling snore can be heard. His lair gives off an eerie red glow and wisps of vapor. Although one of Smaug's drooping eyelids stays open enough to watch for thieves, Bilbo the hobbit is able to sneak in and steal a two-handled cup from the treasure hoard.

ACTUAL SIZE

▶ THE DISCOVERY OF THIS THEFT INFURIATES SMAUG. He circles the sky above the mountain in a rage, bellowing and shooting flames. Later, Bilbo makes himself invisible and sneaks into the dragon's cave again. Although Smaug cannot see Bilbo, he can smell him and he mocks the invisible hobbit. Bilbo flatters the vain Smaug into rolling over onto his back. Bilbo spots an open patch in Smaug's jeweled armor. Knowledge of his weak spot is passed on to Bard the Bowman, who kills Smaug with a single, black, dwarf-made arrow.

Where in the world?

Smaug is the last of the great dragons of Middle Earth in J.R.R. Tolkien's *The Hobbit*. His lair is deep within Lonely Mountain.

Did you know?

- It is unwise to reveal one's true name to a dragon.
- Many experts believe that a dragon is able to breathe fire because it stores a mixture of gases in its body. These gases ignite upon contact with the air, producing an intense flame.
- The dragon's ability to store gases such as methane may account for its terrible stench.
- There is no record of any dragon dying of old age. All dragons in recorded history have died from accidents, disease, or battle injuries.
- Dragons have heightened senses of smell, sight, and hearing. Some breeds can see objects as far as a mile (1.6 km) away and hear sounds well out of the range of the human ear.

Index